T0153308

A Projectile
Point Guide
for the Upper
Mississippi
River Valley

A BUR OAK GUIDE

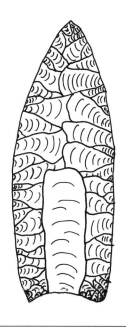

A Projectile
Point Guide
for the Upper
Mississippi
River Valley

Robert F. Boszhardt

University of Iowa Press | Iowa City

University of Iowa Press, Iowa City 52242
Copyright © 2003 by the University of Iowa Press
All rights reserved
Printed in the United States of America

Design by April Leidig-Higgins

http://www.uiowa.edu/uiowapress

No part of this book may be reproduced or used in
any form or by any means without permission in
writing from the publisher. All reasonable steps have
been taken to contact copyright holders of material
used in this book. The publisher would be pleased to
make suitable arrangements with any whom it has
not been possible to reach.

The publication of this book was generously
supported by the University of Iowa Foundation.

Printed on acid-free paper

Library of Congress Cataloging-in-Publication Data
Boszhardt, Robert F.
A projectile point guide for the Upper Mississippi
River Valley / by Robert F. Boszhardt.
p.   cm. — (A Bur Oak guide)
Includes bibliographical references and index.
ISBN 0-87745-870-7 (pbk.)
1. Indians of North America — Implements —
Mississippi River Valley — Guidebooks.   2. Indians
of North America — Mississippi River Valley —
Antiquities — Guidebooks.   3. Projectile
points — Mississippi River Valley — Guidebooks.
4. Mississippi River Valley — Antiquities —
Guidebooks.   I. Title.   II. Series.
E78.M75B67   2003
623.4'41 — dc21   2003050407

03   04   05   06   07   P   5   4   3   2   1

For Andreas and Alianna,
my collecting buddies

Contents

Acknowledgments

This guide would not have been possible with-out the cooperation of hundreds of individual artifact collectors who have shared their artifacts and information with me and my colleagues at the Mississippi Valley Archaeology Center over the past twenty years. No collection is too large or small to be of interest and to make a contribution to understanding our collective heritage. These collections and those recovered by professionals in the region have spawned innumerable discussions with my associates at MVAC and at a variety of institutions throughout the Upper Mississippi Valley, and I appreciate all of the insight. Finally, the compilation of projectile point information was initiated by undergraduate students at the University of Wisconsin–La Crosse nearly fifteen years ago, and reached one level of culmination with an inhouse guide Jeremy Nienow and I prepared around 1995. Other students have since assisted in researching selected point types for independent research projects, and I wish to express my appreciation for their efforts and enthusiasm. Finally, I am most grateful to Brien Woods for his editorial skills and to Danielle Benden for compiling the index on short notice among her many other commitments.

A Projectile Point Guide for the Upper Mississippi River Valley

Introduction

Projectile points are tips fastened to the ends of spears, darts, and arrow shafts. In prehistoric North America, they were made from a variety of materials, including antler, bone, and copper but most, at least most that have been preserved, were made from stone. The vast majority of these were made by chipping various types of "flint" to shape the projectile point for penetration, cutting, and hafting. Projectile point styles changed through time, much like automobiles from the 1920s look different than those from the 1940s, 1960s, or 1990s. Sometimes these changes reflect technological shifts, while other times they appear to be simply fads. In either case, it is somewhat astounding how widespread the use of certain projectile point styles was during particular periods of midwestern prehistory. For example, Paleoindian fluted spear tips, dating between 11,300 and 10,200 years ago (uncalibrated), have been found in every state between the Rocky Mountains and the Atlantic Ocean. Several thousand years later, side-notched forms were being used by Archaic cultures throughout much of eastern North America. At the transition from Archaic to Woodland traditions there was a widespread shift to contracting-stem point types, and toward the end of prehistory virtually every culture adopted unnotched triangular arrow tips.

Although many basic point styles were widespread, they often have a variety of regional names. For example, contracting-stem points are called Waubesa in Wisconsin and the Upper Mississippi Valley, and nearly identical points are called Belknap or Dickson in Illinois and Gary points to the south and east. While there are often modest regional variations in the style with which certain point types were made, there is rarely evidence of individual expression. Point makers in general were conformists and manufactured tips according to prevailing culturally accepted styles. For this reason archaeologists work diligently to develop regional projectile point chronologies for each type that recognize patterns of changing shape through time. These are based on the premise that once a distinct style is directly dated by carbon 14 association, then similar points can be confidently attributed to the same age. All ages included in this guide are uncalibrated. This cross-dating can be applied to points found in excavations, plowed fields, or in private collections.

A number of projectile point guides cover various styles found in the Upper Mississippi Valley. This version is adapted and expanded from a 1995 point guide for western Wisconsin that Jeremy Nienow and I compiled. The drawings in this guide are my own and represent composite styles based on having documented thousands of chipped stone points from this region since 1982. These illustrations do not represent type specimens; however, color photos of selected type examples from the Upper Mississippi Valley may be viewed on the Internet at www.uwlax.edu/mvac. The Internet version also contains links to related sites. Two other recommended print guides that overlap with this area are N. D. Justice's *Stone Age Spear and Arrow Points of the Midcontinental and Eastern United States* and T. A. Morrow's *Iowa Projectile Points*. Several price guides are also available, but most are based on undocumented collections, and all contribute to the destruction of the archaeological record by inevitably disconnecting the locational context from artifacts in their emphasis on selling.

Point typology is a tricky business. We know that basic stylistic patterns changed through time, and we have a fairly good regional chronology of shapes, but many points do not readily conform to "type" examples. Some characteristics, such as corner notching, seem to have been popular during more than one period, so we may need to look for more subtle ways to determine the ages of specific points. Dating points is always a problem with surface finds, yet with avocational and professional archaeologists sharing knowledge, we can detect more precise patterns and associations. Some corner-notched points are found at sites with pottery, others at sites without pottery. Some may be made of heat-treated chert, others of silicified sandstone. Some may have basal grinding, others not. These kinds of attributes can help segregate similar looking points that are from different periods. Sooner or later, each variety will be found in datable contexts, and we will then be able to determine their ages directly. Thus, this point guide will need to be refined and updated, a process made easier through the Internet. You can help with this continual process by recording your finds and letting archaeologists document them through photography and measurements.

Identifying the source of the stone used to manufacture specific points can also be difficult. Some materials such as Knife River flint and jasper taconite are fairly distinctive, and it is generally not difficult to separate Prairie du Chien chert from Galena or Moline cherts. However, nearly all flint sources exhibit stone of considerable variation in color and quality, and there are many look-alikes. For example, until the 1990s nearly every silicified sandstone artifact found in the Upper Mississippi Valley was classified as having been made of material from the well-known Silver Mound source in western Wisconsin. But subsequent identification of numerous other silicified sandstone source areas, including several extensive prehistoric workshops that have produced flakes of color and texture that rival that of Silver Mound, make definitive identifications problematic. Because specific sources are usually from discrete geological formations, fossil inclusions, structural properties, and mineralogical content are useful keys for identification. For example, a distinctive attribute of Burlington chert is the inclusion of fossil crinoids, but these are sometime microscopic. Mineral and structural analyses often require specialized technologies that are generally done at geological laboratories and usually involve partial destruction of a specimen, such as thin sectioning or neutron activation analysis. Fortunately, new and less-destructive analyses are continually being developed. Because of the importance of material identification to understanding past cultural ranges and interaction networks, many professional archaeological institutes have established comparative lithic collections with examples from source areas.

Many people collect spear tips, arrowheads, and other artifacts from plowed fields in the Upper Mississippi Valley. Besides being a pleasant hobby, collecting these artifacts can tell us which culture lived at each site, how old the site is, how people survived, and which trade networks they may have used. Archaeology has a long history of private collectors making significant contributions by sharing their knowledge. Unfortunately, a few untrained people dig into sites or actively buy and sell artifacts, forever destroying critical information needed to interpret the past.

Archaeological sites are nonrenewable resources of our collective heritage. Once destroyed they are gone forever, and with them goes all potential understanding of the past cultures that occupied those sites. In the 130 years from 1850 to 1980 farming, town development, and road construction obliterated nearly 80 percent of the thousands of mounds that once dotted the Upper Mississippi Valley before legislation finally protected those that remained. Now urban sprawl has accelerated the destruction of the irreplaceable archaeological record. It is imperative that we all contribute to preserving as much as possible. Collecting artifacts gives you two options: you can do it ethically and contribute to an understanding of the past, or you can do it selfishly and destroy the record. Note that ethical collecting begins with landowner permission, and it is illegal to collect from any public land, including nearly all of the Upper Mississippi River floodplain. Once permission is obtained from private landowners, you can contribute to archaeological research by following these few simple practices.

Record your find. When you find artifacts, note where you found them as precisely as possible. In the long run, these will be much more valuable to you than a set of artifacts from places long since forgotten. Keep items found at individual sites separate from those found elsewhere. Simple recording systems such as numbering sites works very well. For example, keep all artifacts found on Site 1 together, or label them as such when mixing with others for display. Keeping a notebook with sketch maps of sites is extremely important. An example of a site recording form follows. You could also mark sites on a county map or even a highway map. The best maps are U.S. Geological Survey topographical quadrangles, which are becoming more easily available in digital form through commercial vendors or via the Internet.

For storing, wrap special artifacts separately to prevent them from getting nicked by knocking against other artifacts. Too often, well-intentioned people have dumped coffee cans or old cigar boxes full of artifacts onto our lab tables revealing not only new information but also new breaks and a small pile of fresh chips. Take care of your artifacts; they are a priceless record of the past and are irreplaceable!

Contact an archaeologist. Each state has a state archaeologist, and many colleges and museums have archaeologists who would be happy to photograph your finds and record the information. Rest assured that archaeologists will not confiscate your artifacts, steal your site, or broadcast its location. You will be helping to piece together essential knowledge of the past. In return, you will learn how old your artifacts are, what they are made of, and what they were used for.

Do not buy, sell, or trade artifacts. Buying and selling artifacts not only encourages looting, but once sold, the most important information—site location—is gone forever. It also encourages the manufacture of fraudulent artifacts, and all buyers eventually get taken because fakes can be impossible to distinguish from authentic artifacts. Flintknappers have been producing replicas and fakes for well over a century, and a 1994 survey of modern flintknappers revealed that as many as *1.5 million* replica-fakes are being made *every year*. If you don't know who found it and where it was from, there's a good chance you are buying a fake. As for selling: if you need money that badly, perhaps you should reconsider spending so much time hunting arrowheads.

If you have a collection and you can no longer keep it, either donate it to a state historical society or university with a curation facility, or pass the collection on to the next generation or to someone else who you know will cherish and maintain the collection. This ensures that collection information will follow the actual artifacts. The key is to make sure that information about the material and where it was collected remains with the collection. Donations to non-profit organizations are usually tax-deductible.

Never dig or excavate a site without proper supervision. Archaeological sites cannot be replaced. Once a site is dug improperly, it is destroyed and cannot be reconstructed. There are ample opportunities to participate in professional excavations throughout the Midwest.

Site Recording Form

State Site Code (e.g., 47Lc1)_____ Collector Code (e.g., JD #1)_____

Name: (Landowner) _____ (Contact information:)_____

(Collector)_____ (Contact information:)_____

_____

Site Name: (If the site is not already named, assign one using family name, farm name, landscape feature, etc.) _____

_____

Location and Landscape Description: (Use roads, rivers, buildings, driveways, and any other landmarks. Be as detailed as possible. Use township, range, and section, or even global positioning [GPS] data when possible.) _____

_____

_____

Site Condition: (Type of soil: sandy, clay, silt, etc. Is the area plowed, wooded, pasture, bulldozed, etc.?) _____

_____

_____

Artifact Description: (Points) (If you have a point guide, what do you think it is? What materials are the artifacts made of [i.e., gray chert, white silicified sandstone, etc.]? Trace the outline or draw pictures.) _____

_____

_____

(Ceramics) (Same as above. If you are making a picture, show decorations and note whether the clay is mixed with sand, rock, or shell, and what part of a vessel you think it is from [e.g., rim].) _____

_____

_____

(Other tools) (Drills, knives, pipes, etc.) _____

_____

_____

Additional comments: (This area is available for any other comments that you think would help either in recording the location of or identifying your artifacts. Just make a note of anything that you find interesting or peculiar about your site and/or artifacts.)

_____

_____

_____

(Sketch map and artifact likenesses on reverse)

Point Features and Terminology

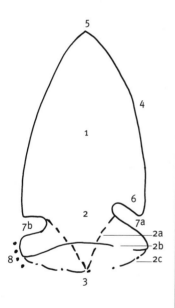

1. Blade: The cutting portion of the point above the hafted stem.
2. Stem: The modified bottom of the blade for hafting onto a shaft or handle.
   a. Contracting: A haft stem that tapers from the shoulder to the base.
   b. Concave: An edge (usually at the base) that curves inward.
   c. Convex: Outward curving edges.
3. Base: The very bottom of the point.
4. Edge: The sides of the blade (may be serrated, beveled [steep angle], pressure flaked, etc).
5. Tip: The pointed top of the blade.
6. Shoulder: The wide portion of the blade immediately above the stem.
7. Notching
   a. Corner-notched: Notches oriented at an upward angle from the basal corners.
   b. Side-notched: Notches oriented perpendicular to the length of the point.
   Another type of notching (not shown), basal-notching, is usually a single notch on the center of the base.
8. Grinding: Edge smoothing on the stem or base to reduce haft splitting and lash cutting. This is common in early spear points.

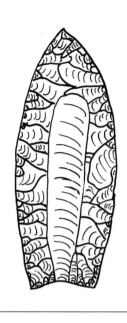

Early Paleo
Fluted Spear
Points

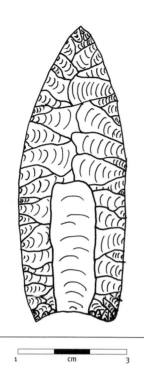

Clovis

1   cm   3

This is the oldest known point type found in North America. This spear point is named after Clovis, New Mexico, where it was found with extinct mammoth bones at Locality 1 of the Blackwater Draw site. Clovis points have also been found in association with mammoths at several sites on the Plains, providing the basis for characterizing Paleoindians as big game hunters.

OTHER POSSIBLE NAMES OR RELATED POINTS: Fluted point, Folsomoid. Goshen points may represent unfluted Clovis points on the basis of having been found beneath Folsom points at the Hell Gap site in Wyoming.

AGE: 11,300 to 10,900 B.P.

DISTRIBUTION: Clovis points are reported from nearly every state south of Canada, suggesting rapid colonization of North America. This type has been found with extinct mammoths and mastodons at several locations in the western and midwestern United States, including the Kimmswick site in Missouri and perhaps the Boaz Mastodon site in Richland County, Wisconsin. A set, or cache, of twenty Clovis-like points was excavated at the Rummells-Maske site in east-central Iowa. Clovis or related fluted points have been found in northern Minnesota and northern Wisconsin, but not above Lake Superior. Those reported from the Upper Mississippi Valley are primarily surface finds from agricultural fields. Goshen points are reported from the northern Plains.

DESCRIPTION: Clovis points are medium to large lanceolate spear-knife points. Their sides are parallel to convex and exhibit careful pressure flaking along the blade edge. The broadest area is near the midsection or toward the base. Bases are distinctly concave with a characteristic flute or channel flake removed from one or, more commonly, both surfaces of the blade. Flutes range from one-quarter to one-half the length of the blade. The lower edges of blade and base are usually ground to dull edges for hafting. Shorter Clovis points are those that have been resharpened until the blade was substantially reduced, and some of these were probably discarded during retooling. Clovis points are distinguished from Folsom points by the relative length of the fluting. Where Clovis points are larger and the channel flake scar typically extends less than halfway up the blade, often terminating in a step fracture, Folsom points are shorter and the flute often runs nearly the entire length of the blade. Clovis points also tend to be thicker than the typically thin Folsom points. Gainey points are longer than Folsom, but also have flutes that extend more than half the blade length. However, some fully fluted points that may be classified as Folsom or Gainey could be resharpened and expended Clovis points.

Length: 4–20 cm/1.5–8 in.   Width: 2.5–5 cm/1–2 in.

MATERIAL: In the Upper Mississippi Valley, these points were often made of high-grade and colorful materials such as fine quality Hixton silicified sandstone or glossy Cochrane chert. Some examples were made of Moline chert (originating from the lower Rock River in Illinois), jasper taconite (from the Thunder Bay area of western Lake Superior), and local Galena and Prairie du Chien cherts. Some Prairie du Chien chert fluted points appear to have been heat-treated.

REFERENCES: Anderson and Tiffany 1972; Bell 1958; Boszhardt 1991; Chapman 1975; Dudzik 1994; Irwin 1968; Justice 1987; Mason 1997; Morrow 1984; Morrow and Morrow 2002; Ritzenthaler 1967; Sellards 1952; Stoltman and Workman 1969.

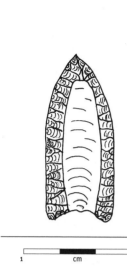

1   cm   3

Folsom/Midland

Folsom points are named after several distinctive points that were found in association with bones of extinct bison in an arroyo near Folsom, New Mexico, in the late 1920s. This find demonstrated for the first time the presence of people in the Americas at the end of the Ice Age and revolutionized North American archaeology. Midland points are named after the Scharbauer sand blow site in Midland County, Texas. Midland-like points were found with Folsom points at the stratified Hell Gap site in Wyoming, but some southern Plains sites have produced only Midland points, suggesting that they date toward the end of the Folsom sequence.

OTHER POSSIBLE NAMES OR RELATED POINTS: Folsom fluted, Folsomoid. Unfluted Folsom-like specimens are called Midland points.

AGE: 10,900 to 10,200 B.P.

DISTRIBUTION: Folsom points are found across the Plains from Texas to Wyoming, often in association with extinct-bison kills. This type extends east to Lake Michigan, mainly north of the Ohio River, but is much less common east of the Mississippi River. Wisconsin appears to be the northeastern extent of its range. These points are rare in the Upper Mississippi Valley, where they have been found only as surface finds thus far. To the east, fully fluted points tend to be larger and are called Gainey.

DESCRIPTION: Folsom points are medium-size, fluted lanceolate spear points. They tend to be very thin and finely made. The broadest section is at or above midsection and the bases are concave. The point is distinguished by channel flake scars that extend nearly the full length of the blade. Edges are resharpened through fine pressure flaking. Basal and lateral edges are typically ground. Length: 4–8 cm/1.5–3 in.   Width: 1.5–4 cm/0.5–1.5 in.

MATERIAL: These points are usually made of high-quality, nonlocal chert types.

REFERENCES: Anfinson 1997; Florin 1996; Mason 1962, 1997; Palmer and Stoltman 1976; Simons et al. 1984; Stoltman 1991; Stoltman and Workman 1969; Wright and Roosa 1966.

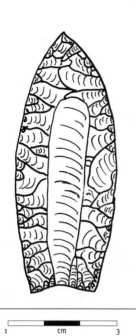

1   cm   3

Eastern Fluted (Gainey)

Fluted points in the region between the Mississippi River and the Atlantic coast are more varied than the Clovis-Folsom sequence on the Plains. A variety of names have been given to these points, including Barnes, Cumberland, Crowfield, Debert, Enterline–Bull Brook, Gainey, and others. Cumberland points tend to cluster in the Southeast, and Debert points are named after the type site in Nova Scotia. A Gainey/Barnes (Parkhill)/Crowfield sequence has been inferred on the basis of site assemblages in the Great Lakes region, although dating is based largely on association with abandoned Great Lakes shorelines. Because the Upper Mississippi Valley is on the eastern margins of the Plains and a relatively short distance from the Great Lakes, it is not surprising that both Plains and eastern fluted point types are reported for this region. Stoltman for instance reclassified fluted points from the Boaz and Withington sites in the Driftless Area as belonging to the Gainey complex. Stoltman did not recognize Barnes or Crowfield points in Wisconsin. Gainey is named after the Gainey site in southeastern Michigan.

OTHER POSSIBLE NAMES OR RELATED POINTS: Barnes, Cumberland, Crowfield, Debert, Enterline–Bull Brook.

AGE: 11,000 to 10,700 B.P.

DISTRIBUTION: Gainey points are found in southern Michigan and Ontario and west to the Mississippi River.

DESCRIPTION: Gainey points are comparable to Clovis in being longer than Folsom. However, whereas channel flake scars on Clovis points do not exceed half the blade length, Gainey points have long, Folsom-like, flutes that run well beyond half the length of the blade. It should be noted that resharpened Clovis points will have longer flute-to-blade ratios, and it is possible to misclassify such points as Gainey. Besides relative flute length, an attribute distinguishing Gainey from Clovis is the preparation of a central basal striking platform for removing the flute in Gainey points. This involves bi-beveled basal preparation that is similar to Folsom technology, which leaves a relatively deep concave base. Gainey points typically display the Barnes finishing technique, which involves post-flute thinning of the base. Blade edges are parallel on most specimens and basal edges are typically ground.

Length: 5–10 cm/2.5–6 in.   Width: 1.5–4 cm/0.5–1.5 in.

MATERIAL: In the Upper Mississippi Valley, fluted points are known to have been made of Hixton silicified sandstone, Cochrane chert, Prairie du Chien chert, Moline chert, and Jasper taconite. Most of these have traditionally been designated Clovis or in a few instances Folsom. More recently, eastern fluted point types have been reported. Stoltman has interpreted the fluted point that was probably found with the Boaz mastodon as a Gainey point. That point is manufactured from Hixton silicified sandstone. Similarly, Stoltman reports that most of the fluted point assemblage from the Withington site in Grant County, Wisconsin, is affiliated with the Gainey complex and most of the fluted points in that assemblage are made of Hixton silicified sandstone, while one is made of quartz and two are made of unidentified chert. A series of Gainey points have been recovered from the Gail Stone site in Trempealeau County, Wisconsin, and these are all made from glossy tan and red Cochrane chert, the same material as the jasper flakes found at Withington. Both Gail Stone and Withington have also produced gray chalcedony flakes, and an unfluted lanceolate blade was found at Gail Stone. The gray chalcedony may be another variety of the Cochrane chert family.

REFERENCES: Boszhardt 1998a, 1991; Deller and Ellis 1984; Ellis and Deller 1986; Florin 1996; Mason 1962, 1997; Palmer and Stoltman 1976; Roosa and Deller 1982; Simons et al. 1984; Stoltman 1991; Wright and Roosa 1966.

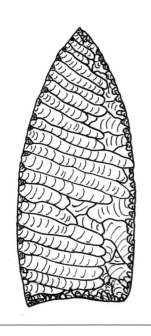

Late Paleo
Lanceolate
Points

1   cm   3

Plainview

Plainview points are named for a series of at least twenty-eight unfluted concave-base lanceolate spear tips found with *Bison antiquus* remains along Running Water Draw near the town of Plainview, in northern Texas. This type has been found at a number of sites on the southern Plains.

OTHER POSSIBLE NAMES OR RELATED POINTS: Goshen points are morphologically similar but are found on the northern Plains and appear to be earlier than the Plainview type. Both are closely related to other unfluted lanceolate points such as Midland.

AGE: Over thirty radiocarbon dates from associated charcoal, bone, and humates range from nearly 12,000 to 8,400 B.P., but stratigraphic data suggest the Plainview type probably was restricted to between about 10,000 and 9,000 B.P. Plainview points were found with Folsom points at Bonfire Shelter, but at Lubbock Lake and several other stratified sites on the southern Plains, they are above Folsom, and therefore later.

DISTRIBUTION: Plainview points are concentrated on the southern Plains, but the type became a catch-all for unfluted lanceolate points throughout the Plains and east into the Upper Mississippi Valley. Stylistically similar Goshen points are clustered on the northern Plains but appear to precede Plainview points by nearly a thousand years. Therefore, unfluted concave-base lanceolate points found in the Upper Mississippi Valley may be the older Goshen points rather than Plainview points, which are moderately rare in this area.

DESCRIPTION: These points are reminiscent of unfluted Clovis points in form. They have parallel sides and shallow concave bases. Basal thinning flakes (multiple miniflutes) are common. Grinding on the lower edges and base is typical. Flaking varies from a fine collateral pattern with a central ridge to a less regular pattern.
Length: 7–12 cm/2.5–5 in.   Width: 2.5–5 cm/1–2 in.

MATERIAL: In the Upper Mississippi Valley, these points are often made of heat-treated, locally available Galena and Prairie du Chien cherts. A few points documented in southwestern Wisconsin are made from Moline chert, imported from the lower Rock River in northwestern Illinois.

REFERENCES: Boszhardt 1991; Bell 1958; Carr 2001; Dudzik 1991; Florin 1996; Hill 1994; Holliday et al. 1999; Justice 1987; Krieger 1947; Mason 1963; Morrow 1984; Ritzenthaler 1967; Sellards et al. 1947; Wormington 1957.

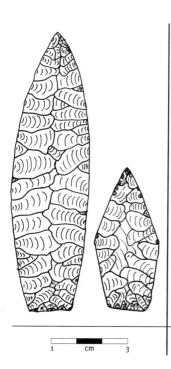

1 cm 3

Agate Basin

This type is named after points found at the Agate Basin site complex in eastern Wyoming. Excavations at this well-stratified site produced multiple point types, including a Folsom/Agate Basin/Hell Gap sequence, each associated with discrete beds of extinct bison bones. The main bison bone bed (Area II) was situated 20 to 30 centimeters above a Folsom level and produced forty-six complete and broken Agate Basin points.

OTHER POSSIBLE NAMES OR RELATED POINTS: Angostura, long or oblique Yuma.

AGE: 10,500 to 10,000 B.P. Charcoal from the Agate Basin component at Area II produced a radiocarbon date of 10,430 ± 570 B.P.

DISTRIBUTION: This type is widespread on the Plains, extending east as far as Ohio and Lake Michigan, and is found on both sides of the upper Mississippi River. East of the Mississippi River, this type is most concentrated in western Illinois and southern Wisconsin.

DESCRIPTION: Medium to large in size, Agate Basin lanceolates were used as spear tips and knives. They are widest at their midsection with convex edges that narrow to the base. Their blades are often carefully flaked in a collateral pattern where the horizontal flake scars meet at a central ridge. Bases are usually straight but may be slightly concave or convex. The lower edges are normally ground heavily, and sometimes the grinding extends nearly 7 centimeters above the base.

Short Agate Basins are often nubs of larger points that were resharpened until the blade was nearly gone, and these may be confused with Hell Gap points. On these discarded points all but the very tip is ground.

Length: 6–15 cm/2.5–6 in.   Width: 2.5–4 cm/1–1.5 in.

MATERIAL: These points are usually made from regionally available cherts such as Galena, Moline, and Burlington, or silicified sandstone. Numerous examples made of Hixton silicified sandstone and nonglossy tan Cochrane chert are known from western Wisconsin. A few Agate Basin points made from exotic flint have also been reported for this region. For example, Hill reports the base of an obsidian specimen from Silver Mound, and Knife River flint specimens are also known from the Upper Mississippi Valley. In addition, a few examples made from jasper taconite and Silurian II chert from Lake Superior and Green Bay, respectively, are known to come from this region.

REFERENCES: Boszhardt 1991; Carr 2001; Chapman 1975; Dudzik 1991; Fishel 1988; Florin 1996; Frison 1991; Frison and Stafford 1982; Halsey 1974a; Hill 1994; Hofman and Graham 2000; Justice 1987; Morrow 1984; Perino 1968; Roberts 1943; Wormington 1957.

1   cm   3

Hell Gap

Named after the Hell Gap site in Wyoming, ten of these points were also associated with extinct bison in Area III of the Agate Basin site complex.

OTHER POSSIBLE NAMES OR RELATED POINTS: These points are sometimes confused with reworked Agate Basin points.

AGE: 10,000 to 9,500 B.P. A charred log from the Hell Gap component at Agate Basin Area III produced a date of 10,445 ± 110 B.P. Hell Gap points are stratigraphically above Folsom points at the Hell Gap site, and Hell Gap associated bone beds are stratigraphically above Folsom and Agate Basin components at the Agate Basin site.

DISTRIBUTION: Hell Gap points are most common on the Plains but may extend to the Upper Mississippi Valley. One Hell Gap point made of Hixton silicified sandstone is reported from the Upper Peninsula of Michigan.

DESCRIPTION: These are finely made, medium-size lanceolate spear-knife points. Hell Gap points expand from the base and constrict toward the tip. The base is normally straight. Grinding of lateral and basal edges is common. Some points that are classified as Hell Gap in the Upper Mississippi Valley may be reworked and expended Agate Basin points.
Length: 6–13 cm/2.5–5.5 in.   Width: 2.5–4 cm/1–1.5 in.

MATERIAL: Some Hell Gap points on the Plains were made from Knife River flint (a semitranslucent brown chalcedony from western North Dakota). Several Hell Gap points, documented from collector territories along the east side of the Upper Mississippi Valley in western Wisconsin, are made of locally available Prairie du Chien chert, while only one was made of Hixton silicified sandstone. A "Hell Gap" point that may be an expended Agate Basin point found near Silver Mound in western Wisconsin was made of Gun Flint silica from the Boundary Waters area west of Lake Superior. The Hell Gap point made from Hixton silicified sandstone from Michigan's Upper Peninsula is nonexpended.

REFERENCES: Agogino 1961; Boszhardt 1991; Carr 2001; Florin 1996; Frison 1991; Hill 1994; Hofman and Graham 2000; Irwin-Williams 1973; Morrow 1984; Perino 1971.

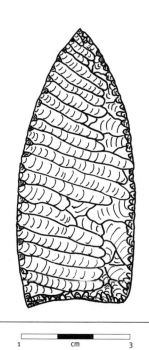

1   cm   3

Frederick/Allen/ Browns Valley

Frederick points were identified at the Hell Gap site in Wyoming. Allen points are named after the Jimmy Allen site, also in Wyoming. Browns Valley points are associated with a burial site in Traverse County in west-central Minnesota.

OTHER POSSIBLE NAMES OR RELATED POINTS: Angostura, and Clary and Clay points from western Nebraska.

AGE: 9,000 to 8,000 B.P. Two samples of human bone collagen from the Browns Valley site were directly dated to 9,000 B.P. The Jimmy Allen site was dated to 8,000 B.P.

DISTRIBUTION: This style is found across the northern Plains from Wyoming to Minnesota, with a few examples reported from the Upper Mississippi Valley, including a chert point found in the Gran Grae valley, Crawford County, Wisconsin.

DESCRIPTION: These are lanceolate spear tips that are similar to Agate Basin points in form. Browns Valley points are somewhat wider. The distinctive characteristic is parallel diagonal, or transverse oblique, flaking across the blade surface that creates a "ripple" effect. These narrow flake scars appear to have been set up so that the manufacturer popped a continuous series of uniform flakes at an oblique angle from the tip that often run across the entire width of the blade. Bases are slightly concave to flat and basal grinding is common.
Length: 3.6–9 cm/1.5–3.5 in.   Width: 3–5 cm/1.5–2 in.

MATERIAL: The six specimens in the Browns Valley type set (four points found with two asymmetrical knives) were all made of Knife River flint from western North Dakota. The Gran Grae specimen is made probably of heat-treated Prairie du Chien chert, which is local to Crawford County.

REFERENCES: Anfinson 1997; Arzigian 1981; Florin 1996; Frison and Stafford 1982; Hofman and Graham 2000; Irwin William et al. 1973; Jenks 1937; Mulloy 1959; Wormington 1957.

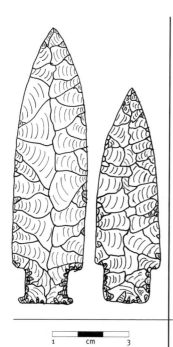

1   cm   3

Eden/Scottsbluff

Eden points (left) were first reported in Yuma County, Colorado, and in undisturbed contexts at the Finley site, near Eden, Wyoming. The Scottsbluff type (right) was named after the Scottsbluff bison kill site in northwest Nebraska. The Firstview complex was suggested for comparable points from the southern Plains based on finds at the Olsen-Chubbuck *Bison antiquus* bone bed.

OTHER POSSIBLE NAMES OR RELATED POINTS: Eden Eared, Scottsbluff Eared (more prevalent in eastern Wisconsin), Scottsbluff Type I and II, Firstview (southern Plains variant).

AGE: 9,200 to 8,800 B.P. on the northern Plains. The Firstview variant is dated to 9,400–8,300 B.P. based on a tight cluster of radiocarbon dates from the Olsen-Chubbuck bone bed in eastern Colorado and similar dated components on the southern Plains.

DISTRIBUTION: Eden points are common on the northern Plains, with examples found from Wyoming to Wisconsin and south as far as eastern Oklahoma. The eared variation is more frequent in eastern Wisconsin but has also been found in northeast Iowa. Scottsbluff points are found throughout the northern Plains. This style becomes rare east of the Mississippi River but is known as far east as Lake Michigan. The eared variety is unknown on the Plains. Scottsbluff points have been found in Late Paleo cremation sites, such as at the Renier site near Green Bay, Wisconsin, and the Gorto site on the Upper Peninsula of Michigan.

Other possible related Late Paleo ritual sites are Pope in central Wisconsin and Deadman Slough in north-central Wisconsin.

DESCRIPTION: These are well-made, medium to long lanceolate spear-knife points. The blade edges are usually parallel with small but angular shoulders. Stems are typically straight but may expand slightly, and some have basal protrusions or ears. The haft stem edges are usually ground. The Scottsbluff type may be confused with examples of straight stemmed, Early Woodland Kramer points. Length: 5–15 cm/2–6 in. (Eden: 3.2–8 in.)   Width: 2.5–4 cm/1–1.5 in.

MATERIAL: In Wisconsin, many of these points are made of Hixton silicified sandstone, but local cherts were also utilized, including Galena and Prairie du Chien cherts along the east side of the Mississippi River. An expended Scottsbluff point made of Hixton silicified sandstone was found in a chipping pile of Galena chert flakes at the Bass workshop site in southwestern Wisconsin.

REFERENCES: Barbour and Schultz 1932; Bell 1958; Boszhardt 1991; Buckmaster and Pauquette 1988; Carr 2001; Dudzik 1991; Florine 1996; Halsey 1974a; Hill 1994; Holliday et al. 1999; Howard 1943; Justice 1987; Luchterhand 1970; Mason 1963, 1997; Meinholtz and Kuehn 1996; Morrow 1984; Perino 1971; Ritzenthaler 1967; Salzer 1974; Wheat 1972; Wormington 1957.

1   cm   3

Dalton/Quad

Dalton points are named after S. P. Dalton, who reported the type site from finds in a Cole County, Missouri, borrow pit. Quad points are named after the Quad site in Alabama.

OTHER POSSIBLE NAMES OR RELATED POINTS: Varieties include Dalton serrated (point sides with serrated edges), Culbert, Greenbrier, and Hardaway. Dalton points also closely resemble Meserve points in size, shape, and quality of construction, resulting in several combinations of names, such as Dalton-Meserve. Quad points, like Suwamee points from Florida, are probably a variant within the Dalton complex.

AGE: 10,000 to 8,000 B.P. Quad points were found in the lowest level of the Graham Cave site in Missouri and were dated to approximately 9,500 B.P.

DISTRIBUTION: Dalton points are found throughout the southeastern and east-central United States, and are concentrated in Arkansas and Missouri. Dalton points are relatively rare in the Upper Mississippi Valley, but several examples have been found in western Wisconsin, southern Minnesota, and north-central Iowa as far west as the Prairie Lakes region. Quad points are most common in northern Alabama, Tennessee, and Kentucky, but a few are reported for the Upper Mississippi Valley. One point from the Itasca Bison Kill site at the headwaters of the Mississippi River resembles Quad, and this site is dated at 10,000–9,000 B.P.

Wilford recovered a Quad-like point from Level 5 of the La Moille Rockshelter site in southeastern Minnesota.

DESCRIPTION: Dalton points are medium to large spear-knife points. The blade is usually well flaked and roughly triangular or lanceolate shaped. Resharpened Dalton knives may exhibit steep beveling on each of the edges. The stem sides are straight or slightly concave, while the base usually is deeply concave and shows fine thinning flakes often resembling short fluting. The base is often ground. Some Dalton points have been resharpened into drills or awls.
Length: 5–8 cm/2–7 in.   Width: 1.5–4 cm/0.5–1.5 in.

MATERIAL: Most examples in western Wisconsin are made of locally available Galena or Prairie du Chien cherts, and some are heat-treated. A few are made of Hixton silicified sandstone or imported Burlington chert.

REFERENCES: Anfinson 1997; Bell 1958; Boszhardt 1991; Carr 2001; Chapman 1948, 1975; Dejarnette et al. 1962; Florin 1996; Goodyear 1982; Justice 1987; Morrow 1984; Morse 1997; Ritzenthaler 1967; Soday 1954.

1   cm   3

Hi-Lo/
Price Stemmed/
Chesrow

Hi-Lo points are named for the Hi-Lo site in western Michigan. Price Stemmed points are named after the Price III site in southwestern Wisconsin. Chesrow points are named after the Chesrow complex in southeastern Wisconsin.

OTHER POSSIBLE NAMES OR RELATED POINTS: One Hi-Lo style variant is described as being relatively short and having expanding sides with basal thinning rather than fluting. Hi-Lo points, along with similar Price Stemmed and some Chesrow points, are probably local variants of Quad points from Michigan, southwestern Wisconsin, and southeastern Wisconsin, respectively.

AGE: A series of Quad (Price/Chesrow) points are documented from Mississippi River islands near Prairie du Chien, Wisconsin. These islands correlate to the Kingston Terrace, which formed sometime after about 12,000 B.P. and was subsequently scoured between 10,500 and 9,200 B.P. Therefore, the points almost certainly postdate 10,000 B.P. Price Stemmed points were initially thought by Freeman and Halsey to date to the Early-Middle Woodland stage. Intensive study near the Kickapoo River subsequently attributed these points to the Late Paleo period. Twelve specimens recovered from the lowest cultural levels excavated at the Bard Lawrence Rockshelter site were stratigraphically beneath Middle-Late Archaic Raddatz points. Faunal analyses from Bard Lawrence found no evidence of occupation during the Pleistocene. Stoltman has equated Price Stemmed and Chesrow points, recognizing several examples from deep cultural levels at other Driftless Area rockshelters. Overstreet suggests that Chesrow points represent a pre-Clovis complex in southeastern Wisconsin, based in part on the proximity to apparently butchered mammoths that have produced dates at 12,000 to 12,500 B.P. However, Chesrow points have not been found at any of the excavated mammoth sites or in any other subsurface contexts in that region. Based on similarities with Quad and Price Stemmed points, Chesrow points probably also reflect Late Paleo activity dating from 10,000 to 9,000 B.P.

DISTRIBUTION: Hi-Lo points are found in Michigan and adjacent Great Lakes states with a few examples reported along the Upper Mississippi Valley into Minnesota. Price Stemmed is the local designation for points found in southwestern Wisconsin, and Chesrow is the designation for those from southeastern Wisconsin.

DESCRIPTION: These points are small to medium spear-knife points that are relatively crude and thick compared to other Late Paleo and Early Archaic types. Blades are usually long and narrow with parallel sides that go to a snub-point tip. These points have shallow concave stems and bases, resulting in varying degrees of basal ears. Shoulders are often barely discernible. Basal grinding occurs on some.
Length: 4–13 cm/1.5–5 in.   Width: 1.5–4 cm/0.5–1.5 in.

MATERIAL: These points tend to be made from local chert sources.

REFERENCES: Boszhardt et al. 1999; Ellis and Deller 1982; Fitting 1963, 1970; Florin 1996; Freeman 1966; Halsey 1974b, 1976; Mason 1997; Overstreet 1993; Sodey 1954; Stoltman 1991.

Early Archaic Stemmed and Corner-Notched Points

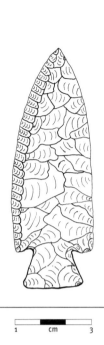

Hardin Barbed

This medium-large spear-knife tip was first recognized as a distinct form in the central Mississippi Valley. The type site is the Godar site, near the town of Hardin in Calhoun County, Illinois.

OTHER POSSIBLE NAMES OR RELATED POINTS: The Hardin Barbed type may have derived from the Scottsbluff type and is related to Thebes and St. Charles points. The type has also been referred to as Hardin and Hardin Stemmed.

AGE: 10,000 to 8,500 B.P. An isolated Hardin Barbed point was found with an extinct peccary tooth at Castle Rock cave in southwestern Wisconsin.

DISTRIBUTION: Hardin Barbed points are found primarily in the Midwest and central Mississippi Valley up into southern Wisconsin. Their range is concentrated between Oklahoma and Indiana. This type is rare north of the Wisconsin River. Numerous Hardin Barbed points were recovered from the Bass site, a prehistoric Galena chert workshop in Grant County, Wisconsin.

DESCRIPTION: These are medium to large spear-knife points. The blades are lanceolate shape to triangular and are often beveled or serrated from resharpening. Shoulders have downward tending barbs formed by an expanding stem. Stems sometimes flare at the base, forming slight ears. Bases are concave to straight. The stem and basal edges are usually ground. These points are rarely heat-treated. Hardin Barbed points are distinguished from the Scottsbluff type by the presence of barbs, serration, and beveling on Hardin specimens.

Length: 3–15 cm/1–6 in.   Width: 3–5 cm/1–2 in.

MATERIAL: Hardin Barbed points found in the Upper Mississippi Valley are often made from Galena or Burlington chert.

REFERENCES: Behm 1985; Bell 1960; Chapman 1975; Justice 1987; Morrow 1984; Scully 1951.

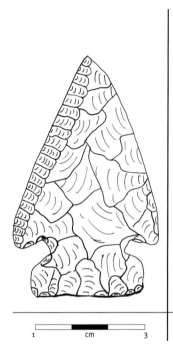

1   cm   3

Thebes

This point type was first recognized as a result of survey work done in the Cache and Wabash valleys of Illinois.

OTHER POSSIBLE NAMES OR RELATED POINTS: Key-Notched Point, Bristol Diagonal-Notched, Cache Diagonal-Notched.

AGE: 10,000 to 8,000 B.P.

DISTRIBUTION: Thebes points are most concentrated in the central Midwest and become rare north of the Wisconsin River.

DESCRIPTION: Thebes points are medium to large spear points or knives with distinctly square notches. Blades are bifacially thinned by percussion flaking. Shoulder barbs are usually rounded. Blades are well made with straight sides, often exhibiting steep, alternate beveling from edge resharpening. Basal edges may be straight or slightly concave or convex. Basal tangs are usually rounded or lobed, and bases are usually ground. Stems are large but not as wide as the shoulders and they are usually heavily ground. Notches are broad and parallel-sided with slight upward angles. Some Thebes points were reworked into scrapers.
Length: 5–16 cm/2–6.5 in.　　Width: 4–9 cm/1.5–3.5 in.

MATERIAL: In the Upper Mississippi Valley, Thebes points tend to be made from Burlington chert, but a few known examples are made from Moline chert, Galena chert, and Hixton silicified sandstone.

REFERENCES: Goldstein and Osborn 1988; Justice 1987; Luchterhand 1970; Palmer 1974; Perino 1971; Winters 1963.

1 cm 3

St. Charles

This point type was named after examples found in central Illinois and eastern Missouri. The type site is the Gronefeld site, St. Charles County, Missouri.

OTHER POSSIBLE NAMES OR RELATED POINTS: Dovetail, Plevna, and Circle-top.

AGE: 10,000 to 8,000 B.P.

DISTRIBUTION: St. Charles points are found throughout the eastern United States and in the Midwest primarily south of the Wisconsin River. A few examples have been found north toward Silver Mound in western Wisconsin as well as in northeastern Iowa and southern Minnesota, including an expended specimen made of Burlington chert that was excavated from the Challey-Turbenson Cedar Valley chert workshop site.

DESCRIPTION: St. Charles points are medium to large spear-knife points. Blades are well made with convex sides, widest at the midsection or toward the shoulder. Points are sometimes unifacially barbed and/or serrated, and well-used points typically have beveled edges from repeated resharpening. Notches are deep and narrow or moderately V-shaped. Stems are generally short and narrow. Bases are usually ground and strongly convex.
Length: 4–10 cm/1.5–4 in. (may extend to 7 in.)   Width: 2.5–5 cm/1–2 in.

MATERIAL: In the Upper Mississippi Valley, some of these points were manufactured from Hixton silicified sandstone and Burlington chert.

REFERENCES: Bell 1960; Chapman 1975; Justice 1987; Luchterhand 1970; Moffat 1996; Morrow 1984; Scully 1951.

1   cm   3

Kessell Side-Notched

This relatively small Early Archaic point type was found in Zone 36 at a depth of 15 to 16 feet at the well-stratified St. Albans site along the Kanawha River valley in West Virginia. It is distinctive for its fine, expanding, puzzlelike notches. Kessell Side-Notched points were found stratigraphically beneath Kirk points at St. Albans. The type is apparently most common in West Virginia and appears sporadically along the Ohio River valley in Pennsylvania, Ohio, Kentucky, and Indiana. It was unrecognized in the Upper Mississippi Valley until recently, as several Kessell-like points have been found in western Wisconsin.

OTHER POSSIBLE NAMES OR RELATED POINTS: This type is apparently ancestral to Kirk Corner-Notched points in West Virginia and is probably related to Cache River points in the lower Mississippi Valley.

AGE: 10,000 to 10,500 B.P. These points were associated with a hearth in Zone 36 at St. Albans, which was dated to 7900 ± 500 B.P. A Kessell point was also found in Early Archaic levels at the Longworth Gick site in Kentucky.

DISTRIBUTION: Kessell Side-Notched points are most common along the central Ohio River valley but extend at least into western Wisconsin. Several are documented from the Kickapoo Valley in southwestern Wisconsin. One is known from De Kalb County in western Illinois. Cache River points are centered in northeastern Arkansas and extend into southeast Missouri, west Tennessee, and northwest Mississippi.

DESCRIPTION: These are relatively small corner-notched points with distinctive puzzlelike notches that are narrow on the blade edge, enlarging into rounded ends. The blades are relatively thin and edges are finely pressure flaked. Edges are slightly convex but taper in from the notches, creating slight, pointed shoulder barbs. Bases are usually concave, forming squarish ears beneath the notches. The base and ears are often ground.

Length: 3.5–5 cm/1.5–2 in.   Width: 2.3–2.9 cm/1–1.5 in.

MATERIAL: In western Wisconsin these points are usually made of heat-treated, locally available Prairie du Chien chert.

REFERENCES: Broyles 1971; Justice 1987; Perino 1971.

1   cm   3

Kirk Corner-Notched

This point type was first recognized in the southeastern United States.

OTHER POSSIBLE NAMES OR RELATED POINTS: Cypress Creek II, Kirk Stemmed, Kirk Serrated. This type evolved from the earlier Palmer Corner-Notched type and may be related to Kessell-like corner-notched points found sporadically in the Driftless Area.

AGE: 9,000 to 7,000 B.P. One nearly complete probable Kirk Corner-Notched point and a basal fragment were found in Feature 3, stratigraphically below most of the Raddatz Side-Notched points at the Raddatz Rockshelter site in Sauk County, Wisconsin. Feature 3 was dated at 5,241 B.P.

DISTRIBUTION: Primarily found in the eastern United States, this type is uncommon along the Upper Mississippi Valley. Several examples, however, have been documented as far north as Buffalo County, Wisconsin.

DESCRIPTION: A spear-knife point. The blade is triangular with a straight or slightly rounded base. Blade edges are sometimes serrated. Shoulders are wide and exhibit barbs projecting down toward the base with deep corner notches. Thin examples with fine notching may be related to Kessel-like points.
Length: 4–10 cm/1.5–4 in.   Width: 2.5–5 cm/1–2 in.

MATERIAL: These points are made primarily of chert.

REFERENCES: Broyles 1971; Coe 1964; Higgins 1990; Justice 1987; Wittry 1959.

Middle Archaic Stemmed and Side-Notched Points

1   cm   3

Matanzas

Matanzas points are named after the West Matanzas site in the central Illinois River valley.

OTHER POSSIBLE NAMES OR RELATED POINTS: Helton, Fishspear, Brunswick. Nearly 250 Matanzas points were found in Helton phase levels at the deeply stratified Koster site in western Illinois, and the type was subdivided into several varieties: Modal, Deep Side-Notched, Faint Side-Notched, Flared Stemmed, Straight Stemmed. The Faint Side-Notched variety may resemble Price Stemmed and Chesrow points, but the base is generally straight as opposed to concave.

AGE: The points are well-dated to 6,000 to 5,000 B.P. (Helton phase) at the Koster site, 5,920 B.P. at the Barton-Milner site in north-central Illinois, 4,780 B.P. at the Murphy site in Dane County, Wisconsin, and 4,330 B.P. at the Crow Hollow site in the Kickapoo Valley of southwestern Wisconsin.

DISTRIBUTION: These points are common in Illinois, Missouri, and eastern Iowa, although they are rare in the northern portion of the Upper Mississippi Valley.

DESCRIPTION: The points are small to medium spear-knife points. Blades are relatively thick, long and narrow with parallel sides that merge at a snub-point tip. They have short stems with shallow side notches, which are never deeper than they are wide. The blade of the Faint Side-Notched Matanzas merges with the stem forming a shallow concave curve. Bases are usually straight or slightly concave and basal ears are small and round. Basal grinding occurs on nearly 60 percent of the specimens.

Length: 4–6 cm/1.5–2.5 in.   Width: 1.5–4 cm/0.5–1.5 in.

MATERIAL: Matanzas points are made from local chert, and heat-treating is common.

REFERENCES: Cook 1976; Justice 1987; Kuehn 1997; Morrow 1984; Munson and Harn 1966; Perino 1968; Stoltman 1997.

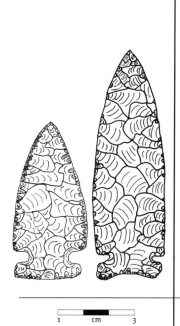

1   cm   3

Raddatz
Side-Notched/
Osceola

These points are named after specimens found at the Raddatz Rockshelter site, Sauk County, Wisconsin, the Osceola site in Grant County, Wisconsin, and at the Airport site near Madison, Wisconsin.

OTHER POSSIBLE NAMES OR RELATED POINTS: Godar. Osceola points (right) are very similar to Hemphill points.

AGE: 5,000 to 3,500 B.P. They are accurately dated stratigraphically below Durst points in several rockshelters and at several open air sites.

DISTRIBUTION: Found throughout the Midwest.

DESCRIPTION: These points are medium-size side-notched spear tips. Blades are triangular to parallel sided, with Osceola predominantly parallel, and converge sharply at the tip. Notches are moderate in size and tend to be U-shaped, inserted at right angles to the blade. Basal ears tend to line up with the blade edges. Bases are slightly concave to straight and are sometimes ground (usually on concave bases). Concave forms tend to be larger and are probably an early variant, having evolved from Early Archaic notched forms. A few serrated or beveled examples are known. Raddatz points (left) with straight or slightly convex bases are generally smaller, and may represent a shift in hunting technology to compound shaft darts. The Madison Side-Notched variant usually has a wide base with shallow side notches just above the base. These points are relatively crude and are best described as wide Raddatz points with shallow side notches. They should not be confused with small, Late Woodland Madison triangular points.

Length: 4–9 cm/1.5–3.5 in.   Width: 3–4 cm/1–1.5 in. (Raddatz)

Length: 9–24 cm/3.5–9.5 in.   Width: 3–4 cm/1–1.5 in. (Osceola)

MATERIAL: In the Upper Mississippi Valley these points are usually made of local chert such as from the Prairie du Chien formation and are often heat-treated, resulting in a lustrous finish.

REFERENCES: Bell 1958; Boszhardt 1977; Justice 1987; Morrow 1984; Ritzenthaler 1967, 1982; Stoltman 1997; Wittry 1959.

Late Archaic
Stemmed and
Corner-Notched
Points

Preston Corner-Notched

This type was defined on the basis of type specimens from the Preston Rockshelter site in the Driftless Area of southwestern Wisconsin.

OTHER POSSIBLE NAMES OR RELATED POINTS: Monona Stemmed, Merom Expanding Stem, Trimble Side-Notched (Wabash Valley), Springly (west-central Illinois).

AGE: 3,500 B.P. Stoltman recognized this type as occurring stratigraphically between the Raddatz and Durst levels at the Preston Rockshelter site and includes Wittry's Monona Stemmed forms from the Raddatz and Durst shelters.

DESCRIPTION: These are small corner-notched to expanding stemmed forms. The blade is more triangular in shape than subsequent Durst points, with a distinctly sharper shoulder. Because of their relatively small size, these might be confused with arrow tips. However, the average weight of Preston points is nearly 4 grams, while late prehistoric arrow tips weigh on average only 1 gram. It is possible that Preston Corner-Notched and equally small Durst Stemmed points (see next entry) represent stone tips for detachable foreshafts of compound spears. Length: 2.5–4.5 cm/1–2 in.   Width: 1.7–2.5 cm/0.75–1 in.

MATERIAL: The points are made from local cherts, sometimes heat-treated.

REFERENCES: Boszhardt 2002; Conrad 1986; Stoltman 1997; Winters 1969.

1   cm   3

Durst Stemmed

This type is named after the Durst Rockshelter site in Sauk County, Wisconsin.

OTHER POSSIBLE NAMES OR RELATED POINTS: Durst Stemmed points resemble Table Rock points. They are a regional variant of the Lamoka type cluster found throughout the northeastern United States.

AGE: 3,000 B.P. These points are well-dated at several Wisconsin rockshelters and a few open-air campsites, stratigraphically above Raddatz Side-Notched points and below layers containing Woodland pottery.

DISTRIBUTION: The type is common in Wisconsin, northern Illinois, and eastern Iowa.

DESCRIPTION: Durst Stemmed points are usually small spear tips with long, slightly expanding stems and rounded shoulders. They are roughly flaked, having a relatively thick body. Bases are usually rounded, with stems accounting for one-half to one-third of the total point length. Stem edges may be ground.
Length: 2.5–5 cm/1–2 in.   Width: 2–4 cm/0.5–1.5 in.

MATERIAL: South of the La Crosse River valley, most are made from Prairie du Chien chert (sometimes heat-treated). North of the La Crosse River, many are made of medium to coarse grained (non-Hixton) silicified sandstones.

REFERENCES: Justice 1987; Morrow 1984; Perino 1971; Ritzenthaler 1967; Stoltman 1997; Wittry 1959.

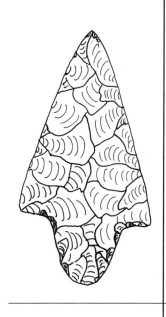

Early Woodland
Stemmed Points

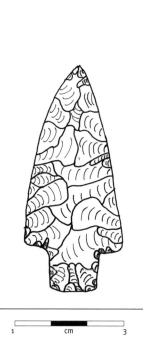

1   cm   3

Kramer

These points are defined from surface associations with the Early Woodland pottery type called Marion Thick found in Illinois.

OTHER POSSIBLE NAMES OR RELATED POINTS: Saratoga point cluster.

AGE: 3,000 to 2,500 B.P. This dating is based on sites in Illinois and Michigan, where Kramer points were associated with Early Woodland Marion Thick pottery. These points are not well dated in the Upper Mississippi Valley.

DISTRIBUTION: Kramer points are found in the Midwest and occasionally along the Upper Mississippi Valley.

DESCRIPTION: The points are medium-size spear points with straight stems. Blades are long with small sloping shoulders. Bases are straight or slightly convex. Basal corners are rounded. Stems are straight and sometimes ground. For this reason they can be confused with Scottsbluff points; however, Scottsbluff points typically exhibit collateral flaking, have sharper shoulders, and almost always have well-ground bases.
Length: 4–9 cm/1.5–3.5 in.   Width: 1.25–2 cm/0.5–1 in.

MATERIAL: These points are almost always made of heat-treated chert.

REFERENCES: Justice 1987; Morrow 1984; Munson 1966, 1971; Perino 1968.

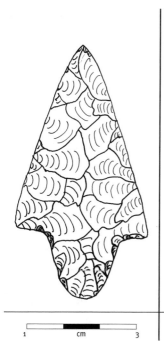

1   cm   3

Waubesa Contracting Stem/ Dickson Broad Blade

Waubesa Contracting Stem points were first recognized at sites near Lake Waubesa, near Madison, Wisconsin. The Dickson Broad Blade variant was subsequently recognized for Illinois.

OTHER POSSIBLE NAMES OR RELATED POINTS: Adena, Belknap, Dickson, Gary, and possibly Mountain Morrow. They are commonly called Beavertails by collectors.

AGE: 2,500 to 1,800 B.P. Earlier interpretations that these points range over several millennia in the upper Midwest were based on surface "associations" with other types. In fact, when found in undisturbed contexts, contracting-stem points in the Midwest are dated to a more restricted period. Waubesa points are well-dated at sealed Early Woodland shell midden sites in the Upper Mississippi Valley, where they are associated with sandy-pasted, Prairie ware ceramics and dated between A.D. 0 and 100. Related Belknap points from Illinois tend to be slightly earlier and are associated with Black Sand pottery. A few contracting-stem points have been recovered from Early-Middle Woodland components in Illinois, dating to ca. A.D. 100.

DISTRIBUTION: These types are found throughout Midwest and are common along the Upper Mississippi Valley.

DESCRIPTION: These points are a medium-size spear type with distinctive contracting stems. Blades are lanceolate to triangular with straight, sloped, or barbed shoulders. Stems are rounded to nearly pointed. Waubesa points are generally smaller and have more pointed stems than Dickson points, and the blades tend to be thick, with minimal evidence of pressure flaking. Most appear to have been percussion flaked as expendable points. The contracting-stem haft element suggests that these were intended for easy removal and replacement. Their increased size from preceding Late Archaic forms may reflect replacement of compound spears (consisting of a main shaft mounted with a foreshaft that was tipped with a relatively small stone point) by arming the main shaft directly with larger, detachable stone tips.

Length: 6–13 cm/2–5 in.   Width: 3–4 cm/1–1.5 in.

MATERIAL: Waubesa points are nearly always made from local chert or silicified sandstone. The less common Adena/Dickson points in the Upper Mississippi Valley are usually made of imported stone including gray "hornstone" (Dongola or Cobdon chert) from southern Illinois or Indiana, Burlington chert from southern Iowa and adjacent portions of Illinois and Missouri, and Knife River flint from North Dakota. These reflect a trade network that is best represented in Red Ocher burials with ceremonial points-knives such as Adena and Turkey Tail. However, some Adena/Dickson points from southern Wisconsin are made of high quality (probably Hixton) silicified sandstone.

REFERENCES: Baerreis 1953a; Boszhardt et al. 1986, 2002; Justice 1987; Morrow 1984; Perino 1971; Ritzenthaler 1967; Theler 1987; Winters 1961.

Middle Woodland
Broad Corner-
Notched Points

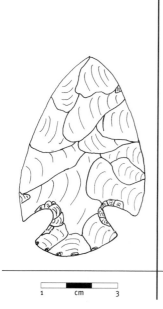

1 cm 3

Snyders Corner-Notched/Manker Corner-Notched

Snyders Corner-Notched points are named after the Snyders site, Calhoun County, Illinois. Manker Corner-Notched points are distinguished from Snyders points in examples found at the Manker site, Illinois.

OTHER POSSIBLE NAMES OR RELATED POINTS: Snyders Notched, Hopewell points.

AGE: 2,200 to 1,800 B.P.

DISTRIBUTION: These points are found throughout the Midwest but are most common in central and northern Illinois, eastern Iowa, southwestern Michigan, eastern Missouri, and southern Wisconsin. They are also known from the Ohio and Mississippi river valleys but are uncommon in the Upper Mississippi Valley. Some examples, however, have been recovered from floodplain islands near Prairie du Chien, Wisconsin, and interior settings such as within the Kickapoo and Root river valleys.

DESCRIPTION: These types are distinctively large, broad corner-notched knives made from oval bifaces. Snyders points are well made with broad bifacial thinning flake scars and convex edges. They tend to be associated with mortuary settings. Manker points are usually less refined, with straighter edges. Shoulders have blunt barbs. Basal edges are convex on Snyders points but may be straight on Manker points. Basal grinding is absent. The notches are broad and oval. Stems are short and only half as wide as the shoulders. A major difference between these two point types is that Snyders points generally have large corner notches and Manker points tend to be more stemmed or open-notched.

Length: 5–15 cm/2–6 in.   Width: 5–10 cm/2–4 in. (Snyder)

Length: 5–10 cm/2–4 in.   Width: 2.5–5 cm/1–2 in. (Manker)

MATERIAL: These points are usually made of flints found in the southern range of the Midwest, such as Burlington chert, although examples made of local Prairie du Chien chert and silicified sandstone have been found in the Upper Mississippi Valley. Snyders points are sometimes heat-treated. Some examples are documented as having been made of Knife River flint, including several associated with Hopewell burial mounds between Prairie du Chien and Trempealeau. Other western exotic flints (including obsidian, speckled [dendritic] jasper, and Morrison siliceous sediment) were also imported and used exclusively for Hopewell mortuary bifaces in this region, and some of these are related to the Snyders type.

REFERENCES: Bell 1958; Boszhardt 1998b; Justice 1987; Logan 1976; McKern 1931; Montet-White 1968; Morrow 1984; Ritzenthaler 1967; Scully 1951; Thomas 1894.

1   cm   3

Steuben Expanded Stemmed/ McCoy Corner-Notched/ Monona Stemmed

Steuben Expanded Stemmed points were first defined at the Steuben site in Illinois. McCoy Corner-Notched points are named after the Silver Creek Site I within the bounds of Fort McCoy in the La Crosse River valley of west-central Wisconsin. Monona Stemmed points are named after the Black Hawk Village site near Lake Monona in Madison, Wisconsin.

OTHER POSSIBLE NAMES OR RELATED POINTS: Steuben points are also known as Lowe Flared Base in southern Illinois, and the type has been divided into three varieties: long and slender, squat and thick, and small and thin. Preston Notched points are similar to Steuben points, and they may be mistaken for one another though Steuben points generally are longer.

AGE: 1,700 to 1,500 B.P. The type is diagnostic of the Millville phase in southwestern Wisconsin.

DISTRIBUTION: Steuben points are common throughout Illinois, Missouri, Iowa, and into southern Wisconsin.

DESCRIPTION: These are small to medium spear points. The blades are triangular with convex edges, and shoulders are straight to sloping. The basal edge is straight to slightly convex while stem edges are concave. Stems expand from the shoulder to the base and account for approximately one-fourth of the point's length. Basal edges are rarely ground. These are sometimes difficult to distinguish from Durst points of the Late Archaic. Both are characterized by expanding stems, but points within the Steuben family usually have sharper shoulders and are made of chert, whereas Durst points tend to have rounded shoulders and may be made of chert or silicified sandstone.

Length: 3–10 cm/1.5–4 in.   Width: 2.5–4 cm/1–2 in.

MATERIAL: These points are typically made of local cherts that may be heat-treated.

REFERENCES: Baerreis 1953b; Boszhardt 1986; Freeman 1969; Hurley 1974; Justice 1987; Morrow 1984; Perino 1971; Ritzenthaler 1967; Theler 1987; Winters 1961.

Late Prehistoric
Woodland
and Oneota
Arrowheads

1   cm   3

Honey Creek Corner-Notched

Honey Creek Corner-Notched points appear to represent the first true arrowhead form in the Upper Mississippi Valley. This type was defined after work at the Rehbein Mounds in Richland County, Wisconsin, and comparison with points from several other sites. The Honey Creek name was derived from the creek that flows near the Durst Rockshelter. A point associated with a linear mound burial on Picnic Point in Madison is probably within the range of this type.

OTHER POSSIBLE NAMES OR RELATED POINTS: Klunk, Koster, Scallorn, and possibly Reed. This point type replaced the Small Diagonal-Notched category reported in several southwestern Wisconsin rockshelters and is similar in shape to Preston Corner-Notched and Monona/Steuben Stemmed types, though the points are generally smaller and distinctly lighter; they nearly always weigh less than 2 grams.

AGE: 1,700 (?) to 1,200 B.P. These points have been found in levels with Madison triangular points at the Durst Rockshelter site. They are associated with Linn ware ceramics of the Millville phase at several sites. They are found in both conical and linear mounds in the Kickapoo Valley, including Mounds 3 and 5 at the Rehbein. Mound 3, a conical, was dated to 1,850 to 1,700 B.P. Mound 5, a linear, was dated at 1,300 to 1,200 B.P. One example was found in a layer at Hadfields Cave in northeastern Iowa that was dated to 1,450 to 1,200 B.P.

DISTRIBUTION: Honey Creek points are somewhat common in the Upper Mississippi Valley.

DESCRIPTION: These small "diagonally notched" points have straight or slightly convex edges. Bases are straight to slightly convex and may be flared, while notches are small. While most are bifacial, some are simply flakes that were retouched into points with corner notches. These points may sometimes be confused with Monona Stemmed/McCoy Corner-Notched/Steuben Expanding Stemmed, but Monona Stemmed and Steuben Expanding Stemmed are 25 percent larger and have broader notches and a base with a more pronounced flare.
Length: 1–3 cm/0.5–1.5 in.   Width: 1.25–2 cm/0.5–1 in.

MATERIAL: These points are usually made of local chert.

REFERENCES: Benn 1980; Mead 1979; Wittry 1959.

Cahokia/Grant Side-Notched

1   cm   3

The Cahokia point type is named after the major Middle Mississippian Cahokia site near St. Louis.

OTHER POSSIBLE NAMES OR RELATED POINTS: Grant Side-Notched and Prairie du Sac Notched in southwestern Wisconsin. Cahokia counterparts on the Plains are Washita, Harrel, and Reed points. Similar to Huffaker points, the basic Cahokia preform also resembles the Madison type in manufacture.

AGE: These points represent a horizon marker from 1,000 to 850 B.P., representing Middle Mississippian/Cahokia and related site complexes (e.g., Steed Kisker, Mill Creek, terminal Late Woodland [Effigy Mound], and Early [Emergent] Oneota).

DISTRIBUTION: Illinois, Iowa, southern Wisconsin, Missouri, northern Arkansas, and eastern Oklahoma.

DESCRIPTION: This type has been segregated into four subclasses: Cahokia double-notched, triple-notched, multiple-notched, and serrated. The points are small to medium arrow tips. They are thin and generally well-made with either straight or triangular converging sides. This family exhibits multiple notching patterns, but characteristically they have a pair of relatively deep side notches. Cahokia double-notched are the most common Cahokia type found in the Upper Mississippi Valley. Triple-notched points are rare in the Upper Mississippi Valley.

One point, found at the Energy Park site, an Early Oneota village near Red Wing, Minnesota, has five notches: two on each side and one in the center of the base. At the blended Late Woodland–Middle Mississippian Fred Edwards site in Grant County, Wisconsin, side-notched triangular points were distinguished from Grant Side-Notched on the basis of the angle of the base. Grant Side-Notched points have a square base with a 90-degree angle. Other side-notched triangular points have basal angles less than 90 degrees. Both Grant points and side-notched triangular points were recovered in number at the Fred Edwards site, which is well-dated between A.D. 1050 and 1150. Finney and Stoltman also isolate the Prairie du Sac Side-Notched variety as having a base that is narrower than the shoulder. This subtype may be related to Honey Creek Corner-Notched points; however, only one was found at the Fred Edwards site. Length: 1.5–3.5 cm/0.7–1.75 in.   Width: 1.3–2 cm/0.6–1 in.

MATERIAL: Cahokia points are nearly always made of local cherts. Only a few examples of silicified sandstone Cahokia points are known for the Upper Mississippi Valley (e.g., the Emergent Oneota, Diamond Bluff/Mero site), including the northern portion, where numerous sources of this material exist. Heat-treatment may occur.

REFERENCES: Finney 1991; Finney and Stoltman 1991; Justice 1987; Morrow 1984; Ritzenthaler 1967; Scully 1951; Stoltman 1993; Titterington 1938.

1   cm   3

Madison Triangular

This point type was first named in an unpublished guide to central Mississippi Valley projectile point types based on examples found at the Cahokia site and in St. Clair and Madison counties, Illinois.

OTHER POSSIBLE NAMES OR RELATED POINTS: Triangular, Fresno, Sanders Triangular, also called bird points by collectors.

AGE: 1,100 to 300 B.P. These points are associated with Late Woodland cultures and the Mississippian/Oneota Traditions.

DISTRIBUTION: Madison points are common throughout the Midwest, concentrated along the Mississippi River basin and Oneota settlement localities.

DESCRIPTION: These are small unnotched triangular points. The blade edges tend to be straight but may be slightly concave or convex. Bases may also vary from straight to concave or convex. Madison points tend to be half as wide as they are long (isosceles triangle), but some are as wide as they are long (equilateral triangle). Although one of many small point styles that are commonly called bird points, these are true arrowheads that were used to hunt game like deer, elk, and bison. These points are made of whatever local lithic materials were available including Prairie du Chien chert and silicified sandstones from the Upper Mississippi Valley. The majority of the Madison points at the Late Woodland/Middle Mississippian village of Aztalan in southeastern Wisconsin, however, are made of silicified sandstone from west-central Wisconsin. A few quartz Madison points have also been found in the Upper Mississippi Valley, having originated in glaciated northern regions. Variations range from nicely made triangles to simple retouched flakes barely recognizable as points. In central Wisconsin, Late Woodland Madison points tend to be serrated and made of silicified sandstone. At Late Woodland (Eastman phase) sites near Prairie du Chien, only a few points are serrated and most are made of local chert. At La Crosse Oneota sites, these points are never serrated and from A.D. 1300 to 1400 were made predominately of silicified sandstone but thereafter were made from chert. It appears that late Oneota points are slightly larger.

Experimental replication of arrows such as those found in the Upper Mississippi Valley indicates that shaft production is a long and laborious task. In contrast, manufacture of unnotched triangular points is relatively simple. The absence of notching suggests that these expedient points were hafted in a fashion that allowed the point to be detached, staying in the wound, while the shaft may have been retrieved and retipped. This would have been an effective weapon, where extraction of the tip may not have been possible by pulling out the shaft. Length: 1.5–3 cm/0.75–2 in.   Width 1.25–2.5 cm/0.5–1 in.

MATERIAL: These points are made from a variety of local and nonlocal materials. In the Upper Mississippi Valley, Madison points are made of Prairie du Chien chert, Galena chert, Hixton and related silicified sandstones, and quartz.

REFERENCES: Justice 1987; Morrow 1984; Perino 1968; Ritzenthaler 1976; Scully 1951.

Bibliography

Agogino, G. A.
1961   A New Point Type from Hell Gap Valley, Eastern Wyoming. *American Antiquity*
       26(4):558–560.

Anderson, A. D., and J. A. Tiffany
1972   Rummells-Maske: A Clovis Find Spot in Iowa. *Plains Anthropologist* 17:55–59.

Anfinson, S. F.
1997   *Southwestern Minnesota Archaeology: 12,000 Years in the Prairie Lake Region.*
       Minnesota Prehistoric Archaeology Series 14. Minnesota Historical Society, St.
       Paul.

Arzigian, C. M.
1981   The Archaeology of Gran Grae: A Survey of the Valley and Headlands of a
       Small Stream in the Driftless Area, Crawford County, Wisconsin. *Wisconsin
       Archeologist* 62(2):207–246.

Baerreis, D. A.
1953a The Airport Village Site, Dane County. *Wisconsin Archeologist* 34(3):149–164.
1953b Blackhawk Village Site, Dane County. *Journal of the Iowa Archeological Society*
       2(4):5–20.

Barbour, E. H., and C. B. Schultz
1932   The Scottsbluff Bison Quarry and Its Artifacts. *Nebraska State Museum Bulletin*
       34(1).

Behm, J. A.

1985   A Stylistic Analysis of Hardin Barbed Points. Ph.D. dissertation, Department of Anthropology, University of Wisconsin–Madison.

Bell, R. E.

1958   Guide to the Identification of Certain American Indian Projectile Points. *Special Bulletin* No. 1, Oklahoma Anthropological Society, Oklahoma City.

1960   Guide to the Identification of Certain American Indian Projectile Points. *Special Bulletin* No. 2, Oklahoma Anthropological Society, Oklahoma City.

Benn, D. W.

1980   *Hadfields Cave: A Perspective on Late Woodland Culture in Northwestern Iowa.* Report 13, Office of the State Archaeologist, University of Iowa, Iowa City.

Boszhardt, R. F.

1977   Wisconsin Radiocarbon Chronology, 1976: A Second Compilation. *Wisconsin Archeologist* 58(2):87–143.

1982   Wisconsin Radiocarbon Compilation Update, 1981, Mississippi Valley Archaeology Center, Inc. *Wisconsin Archeologist* 63(2):128–152.

1991   Paleoindian Study Unit for Region 6, Western Wisconsin. *Wisconsin Archeologist* 72(3–4):155–200.

1998a   Newly Discovered Lithic Resources in Western Wisconsin. *Minnesota Archaeologist* 57:85–96.

1998b   Additional Western Lithics for Hopewell Bifaces in the Upper Mississippi River Valley. *Plains Anthropologist* 43(165):275–286.

2002   Contracting Stemmed: What's the Point. *Midcontinental Journal of Archaeology* 27(1):35–67.

Boszhardt, R. F., W. K. Holtz, and B. J. Bielefeldt

1999   National Register form, Kickapoo Valley Archaeological District. Copy on file, Mississippi Valley Archaeology Center, University of Wisconsin–La Crosse.

Boszhardt, R. F., J. L. Theler, and T. Kehoe

1986   Early Woodland Stage. *Wisconsin Archeologist* 67(3-4):243–262.

Broyles, B. J.

1971   Second Preliminary Report: The St. Albans Site, Kanawha County, West Virginia. *West Virginia Geological and Economic Survey Report Archaeological Investigations* 3.

Buckmaster, M. M., and J. R. Paquette

1988   The Gorto Site: Preliminary Report on a Late Paleo-Indian Site in Marquette County, Michigan. *Wisconsin Archeologist* 69(3):101–124.

Chapman, C. H.

1948   A Preliminary Survey of Missouri Archaeology, Part IV. *Missouri Archaeologist* 10(4):135–164.

1975   *The Archaeology of Missouri.* University of Missouri Press, Columbia.

Coe, J. L.

1964   The Formative Cultures of the Carolina Piedmont. *Transactions of the American Philosophical Society* 54, Part 5, Philadelphia.

Conrad, L. A.

1986   The Late Archaic–Early Woodland Transition in the Interior of West-Central Illinois. In *Early Woodland Archaeology*, edited by K. B. Farnsworth and T. E. Emerson, 301–325. Kampsville Seminars in Archaeology, No. 2, Center for American Archaeology Press, Kampsville, Illinois.

Cook, T. G.

1976   Koster: An Artifact Analysis of Two Archaic Phases in West-Central Illinois. *Northwestern Archeological Program, Prehistoric Records* 1.

DeJarnette, D. L., E. B. Kurjack, and J. W. Cambron

1962   Stanfield-Worley Bluff Shelter Excavations. *Journal of Alabama Archaeology* 8(1&2).

Deller, D. B., and C. J. Ellis

1984   Crowfield: A Preliminary Report on a Probable Paleo-Indian Cremation in Southwestern Ontario. *Archaeology of Eastern North America* 12:41–71.

Dudzik, M. J.

1991   First People: The Paleoindian Tradition in Northwestern Wisconsin. *Wisconsin Archeologist* 72(3-4):137–154.

Ellis, C. J., and D. B. Deller

1982   Hi-Lo Materials from Southwestern Ontario. *Ontario Archaeology* 38:3–22.
1986   Post-Glacial Lake Nipising "Waterworn" Assemblages from the Southeastern Huron Basin Area. *Ontario Archaeology* 45:39–60.

Fiedel, S. J.

1999   Older Than We Thought: Implications of Collected Dates for Paleoindians. *American Antiquity* 64(1):95–115.

Figgins, J. D.

1934   Folsom and Yuma Artifacts. *Proceedings of the Colorado Museum of Natural History* 13(2).

Finney, F. A

1991   Cahokia's Northern Hinterland as Viewed from the Fred Edwards Site in Southwestern Wisconsin: Examining the Evidence for Central Control and Prestige Goods Economy. Ph.D. dissertation, University of Wisconsin–Madison.

Finney, F. A., and J. B. Stoltman

1991   The Fred Edwards Site: A Case of Stirling Phase Culture Contact in Southwestern Wisconsin. In *New Perspectives on Cahokia: Views from the Periphery*, edited by J. B. Stoltman, 229–252. Prehistory Press, Madison, Wisconsin.

Fishel, R. L.

1988 Preliminary Observations on the Distribution of the Agate Basin Point East of the Mississippi River. *Wisconsin Archeologist* 69(3):125–138.

Fitting, J. E.

1963 The Hi-Lo Site: A Late Paleo-Indian Site in Western Michigan. *Wisconsin Archeologist* 44(2):89–96.

1970 *The Archaeology of Michigan: A Guide to the Prehistory of the Great Lakes Region.* Natural History Press, Garden City, New York.

Florin, F.

1996 Late Paleo-Indians of Minnesota and Vegetation Changes from 10,000–8,000 B.P. Master's thesis, University of Minnesota, Minneapolis.

Freeman, J. E.

1966 Price Site III, RI 4, A Burial Ground in Richland County, Wisconsin. *Wisconsin Archeologist* 47(2):41–44.

1969 The Millville Site, a Middle Woodland Village in Grant County, Wisconsin. *Wisconsin Archeologist* 50(2):37–87.

Frison, G. C.

1991 *Prehistoric Hunters of the High Plains,* 2nd ed. Academic Press, San Diego.

Frison, G. C., and D. J. Stafford

1982 *The Agate Basin Site: A Record of the PaleoIndian Occupation of the Northwestern High Plains.* Academic Press, New York.

Goldstein, L. G., and S. K. Osborn

1988 *A Guide to Common Prehistoric Projectile Points in Wisconsin.* Milwaukee Public Museum, Milwaukee.

Goodyear, A. C.

1982 The Chronological Position of the Dalton Horizon in the Southeastern United States. *American Antiquity* 47:382–395.

Halsey, J. R.

1974a The Markee Site (47Ve-195): An Early-Middle Archaic Campsite in the Kickapoo River Valley. *Wisconsin Archeologist* 55(1):42–75.

1974b Gillen 9 (47Ve-177): An Archaic-Woodland Campsite in the Kickapoo River Valley. *Wisconsin Archeologist* 55(3):178–217.

1976 Bard Lawrence I Rockshelter (47Ve-154) in *Report on the Archaeological Investigations in the La Farge Lake Project Area, 1973 and 1974 Seasons,* 118–168. State Historical Society of Wisconsin, Madison.

Higgins, M. J., et al.

1990 The Nochta Site: The Early, Middle, and Late Archaic Occupations. *American Bottom Archaeology, FAI-270 Site Reports,* Vol. 21. University of Illinois Press, Chicago.

Hill, M. G.

1994 Paleoindian Projectile Points from the Vicinity of Silver Mound (47Ja21),

Jackson County, Wisconsin. *Midcontinental Journal of Archaeology* 19(2):223–259.

Hofman, R. W., and J. L. Graham
2000   The Paleo-Indian Cultures of the Great Plains. In *Archaeology on the Great Plains*, edited by W. R. Wood, 87–139. University Press of Kansas.

Holliday, V. T., E. Johnson, and T. W. Stafford
1999   AMS Radiocarbon Dating of the Type Plainview and Firstview (Paleoindian) Assemblages: The Agony and the Ecstasy. *American Antiquity* 63(3): 444–454.

Howard, E. B.
1943   The Finley Site: Discovery of Yuma Points, In Situ, Near Eden, Wyoming. *American Antiquity* 13(3):244–295.

Hurley, W. M.
1974   Silver Creek Woodland Sites, Southwestern Wisconsin. *Office of the State Archaeologist Report* 6. University of Iowa, Iowa City.

Irwin, H. T.
1968   The Itama: Early Late Pleistocene Inhabitants of the Plains of the United States and Canada and the American Southwest. Ph.D. dissertation, Department of Anthropology, Harvard University, Cambridge, Massachusetts.

Irwin-Williams, C. H., G. Agogino, and C. V. Haynes
1973   Hell Gap: Paleo-Indian Occupation on the High Plains. *Plains Anthropologist* 18 (59):40–53.

Jenks, A. E.
1937   Minnesota's Browns Valley Man and Associated Burial Artifacts. *American Anthropological Association Memoir* 40.

Justice, N. D.
1987   *Stone Age Spear and Arrow Points of the Midcontinental and Eastern United States: A Modern Survey and Reference.* Indiana University Press, Bloomington.

Krieger, A. D.
1947   Certain Projectile Points of the Early American Hunters. *Bulletin of the Texas Archaeological and Paleontological Society* 18:7–27.

Kuehn, S. R.
1997   *Archaeological Investigations at the Bell Center Wetland Mitigation Area, Crawford County, Wisconsin.* Research Report No. 63, Museum Archaeology Program, State Historical Society of Wisconsin, Madison.

Logan, W. D.
1976   *Woodland Complexes in Northeastern Iowa.* Publications in Archaeology, No. 15. U.S. Department of the Interior, National Park Service. Washington, D.C.

Luchterhand, K.

1970   Early Archaic Projectile Points and Hunting Patterns in the Lower Illinois Valley.
        Report of Investigations 19, Illinois State Museum, Springfield.

Mason, R. J.

1962   The Paleo-Indian Tradition in Eastern North America. *Current Anthropology*
        3:227–278.

1963   Two Late Paleo-Indian Complexes in Wisconsin. *Wisconsin Archeologist*
        44(4):199–211.

1997   The Paleo-Indian Tradition. *Wisconsin Archeologist* 78(1-2):78–111.

McKern, W. C.

1931   A Wisconsin Variant of the Hopewell Culture. *Bulletin of the Public Museum of
        the City of Milwaukee* 10(2):185–328.

Mead, B.

1979   The Rehbein I Site: A Multi-Component Site in Southwestern Wisconsin.
        Wisconsin Archeologist 60(2):91–182.

Meinholtz, N. M., and S. R. Kuehn

1996   *The Deadman Slough Site.* Archaeological Research Series 4, Museum
        Archaeology Program, State Historical Society of Wisconsin, Madison.

Moffat, C. R.

1996   Archaeological Data Recovery at the Challey/Turbenson Site (21Fl71) and the
        Mundfrom/Till Site (21Fl73), Fillmore County, Minnesota. Reports of
        Investigation No. 220, Mississippi Valley Archaeology Center, University of
        Wisconsin–La Crosse.

Montet-White, A.

1968   The Lithic Industries of the Illinois Valley in the Early and Middle Woodland
        Period. *Anthropological Papers*, No. 35, Museum of Anthropology, University of
        Michigan, Ann Arbor.

Morrow, J. E., and T. A. Morrow

2002   Rummells-Maske Revisited: A Fluted Point Cache from East Central Iowa.
        Plains Anthropologist 47:307–322.

Morrow, T. A.

1984   *Iowa Projectile Points.* Special Publication, Office of the State Archaeologist,
        University of Iowa, Iowa City.

Morse, D. F.

1963   The Steuben Village and Mounds, A Multi-Component Late Hopewell Site in
        Illinois. *Anthropological Papers*, No. 21, Museum of Anthropology, University of
        Michigan, Ann Arbor.

1997   *Sloan: A Paleoindian Dalton Cemetery in Arkansas.* Smithsonian Institution
        Press, Washington, D.C.

Mulloy, W.

1959 The James-Allen Site, Near Laramie, Wyoming. *American Antiquity* 25(1):112–116.

Munson, P. J.

1966 The Sheets Site: A Late Archaic–Early Woodland Occupation in West-Central Illinois. *Michigan Archaeologist* 12(3):111–120.

1971 An Archaeological Survey of the Wood River Terrace and Adjacent Bottoms and Bluffs in Madison County, Illinois. *Illinois State Museum Reports of Investigations*, No. 21, Part 1.

Munson, P. J., and A. D. Harn

1966 Surface Collections from Three Sites in the Central Illinois River Valley. *Wisconsin Archeologist* 47(3):152–153.

Overstreet, D. F.

1993 *Chesrow: A Paleoindian Complex in the Southern Lake Michigan Basin.* Great Lakes Archaeological Press, Milwaukee.

Palmer, H. A.

1974 Implications of an Extinct Peccary–Early Archaic Artifact Association from a Wisconsin Cave. *Wisconsin Archeologist* 55(3):218–230.

Palmer, H. A., and J. B. Stoltman

1976 The Boaz Mastodon: A Possible Association of Man and Mastodon in Wisconsin. *Midcontinental Journal of Archaeology* 1(2):163–177.

Perino, G.

1968 Guide to the Identification of Certain American Indian Projectile Points. *Special Bulletin*, No. 3, Oklahoma Anthropological Society, Oklahoma City.

1971 Guide to the Identification of Certain American Indian Projectile Points. *Special Bulletin*, No. 4, Oklahoma Anthropological Society, Oklahoma City.

Ritzenthaler, R. E.

1946 The Osceola Site: An Old Copper Site near Potosi, Wisconsin. *Wisconsin Archeologist* 27(3):53–70.

1967 A Guide to Wisconsin Indian Projectile Point Types. *Popular Science Series* 11, Milwaukee Public Museum, Milwaukee.

Roberts, F. H., Jr.

1943 A New Site. *American Antiquity* 8(3):300.

Roosa, W. B., and D. B. Deller

1982 The Parkhill Complex and Eastern Great Lakes Paleo-Indians. *Ontario Archaeology* 37:3–15.

Salzer, R. J.

1974 The Wisconsin North Lakes Project: A Preliminary Report. In *Aspects of Upper Great Lakes Anthropology: Papers in Honor of Lloyd A. Wilford*, edited by E. Johnson, 40–54. Minnesota Prehistoric Archaeology Series No. 4, Minnesota Historical Society, St. Paul.

Scully, E. G.

1951   Some Central Mississippi Valley Projectile Point Types. Mimeographed
        manuscript, Museum of Anthropology, University of Michigan, Ann Arbor.

Sellards, E. H.
1952   *Early Man in America.* University of Texas Press, Austin.

Sellards, E. H., G. L. Evans, and G. E. Meade
1947   Fossil Bison and Associated Artifacts from Plainview, Texas. *Geological Society
        of America Bulletin* 58:927–954.

Simons, D. B., M. J. Shott, and H. T. Wright
1984   The Gainey Site: Variability in a Great Lakes Paleo-Indian Assemblage.
        Archaeology of Eastern North America 12:266–279.

Soday, F. J.
1954   The Quad Site, A Paleo-Indian Village in Northern Alabama. *Tennessee
        Archaeologist* 10(1):1–20.

Stoltman, J. B.
1990   The Woodland Tradition in the Prairie du Chien Locality. *The Woodland
        Tradition in the Western Great Lakes,* edited by Guy E. Gibbon, Publications in
        Anthropology, No. 4, University of Minnesota.
1991   1990–1991 Annual Report for Region 8. *State of Wisconsin Regional Archaeology
        Program, State Regional Archaeology Center,* No. 8, Laboratory of Archaeology,
        Department of Anthropology, University of Wisconsin–Madison.
1997   The Archaic Tradition. *Wisconsin Archeologist* 78(1/2):112–139.

Stoltman, J. B., and W. K. Workman
1969   A Preliminary Study of Wisconsin Fluted Points. *Wisconsin Archeologist*
        50(4):189–214.

Theler, J. L.
1987   Woodland Tradition Economic Strategies: Animal Resource Utilization in
        Southwestern Wisconsin and Northeastern Iowa. Report 17. Office of the State
        Archaeologist, University of Iowa, Iowa City.

Theler, J. L., and R. F. Boszhardt
2003   *Twelve Millennia: The Archaeology of the Upper Mississippi River Valley.*
        University of Iowa Press, Iowa City.

Thomas, C. A.
1894   Report on the Mound Explorations of the Bureau of Ethnology. *Twelfth Annual
        Report of the Bureau of American Ethnology, 1890–1891.* Smithsonian Institution,
        Washington, D.C.

Titterington, P. F.
1938   *The Cahokia Mound Group and Its Village Site Materials.* St. Louis.

Wheat, J. B.

1972   *The Olsen-Chubbuck Site: A Paleoindian Bison Kill.* American Antiquity Memoir, No. 26.

Winters, H. D.

1961   The Adler Mound Group, Will County, Illinois. *Chicago Area Archaeology*, Bulletin #3, Illinois Archaeological Survey, University of Illinois, Urbana.

1963   An Archaeology Survey of the Wabash Valley in Illinois. *Illinois State Museum, Reports of Investigations*, No.10.

1969   *The Riverton Culture.* Reports of Investigations, No. 13, Illinois State Museum and Monograph 1, Illinois Archaeological Survey, Springfield.

Wittry, W. L.

1959   Archeological Studies of Four Wisconsin Rockshelters. *Wisconsin Archeologist* 40(4):137–267.

Wormington, H. M.

1957   Ancient Man in North America. *Popular Series 4.* Denver Museum of Natural History, Denver.

Wright, H. T., and W. B. Roosa

1966   The Barnes Site: A Fluted Point Assemblage from the Great Lakes Region. *American Antiquity* 31:850–860.

Index